HORSE

Elizabeth J. Baldwin

CLASH

by ticktock

Copyright © ticktock Entertainment Ltd 2009

First published in Great Britain in 2009 by ticktock Media Ltd,
The Old Sawmill, 103 Goods Station Road, Tunbridge Wells, Kent, TN1 2DP

project editor and picture researcher: Ruth Owen
ticktock project designer: Simon Fenn

Thank you to Lorraine Petersen and the members of nasen

ISBN 978 1 84696 941 6 pbk

Printed in China

A CIP catalogue record for this book is available from the British Library.

Picture credits (t=top; b=bottom; c=centre; l=left; r=right):
AFP/Getty Images: 24t. Bongarts/Getty Images: 22, 23t, 24. Bridgeman Art Library, London/SuperStock: 6t. British
Horse Loggers (http://www.britishhorseloggers.org): 15t. David Burton/FLPA: 8. Corbis: 19t. Getty Images: 12, 13,
17, 23b. Robert Harding World Imagery/Corbis: 6b. iStock: 7. National Geographic/Getty Images: 18-19.
Photograph by Austin Hargrave; courtesy of Michael Goessling (http://www.worldssmallesthorse.com): 10b. Priefert
Percherons: 11. Lisa Ross-Williams (If Your Horse Could Talk/Equi-Spirit Toys and Tools): 28-29, 29. Ron
Sachs/CNP/Corbis: 16. Shutterstock: OFC, 1, 2-3, 4-5, 6 (background), 8-9, 9t, 10t, 14-15, 20-21, 22-23
(background), 25, 26-27 (background), 26, 27t, 27b, 31.

Every effort has been made to trace copyright holders, and we apologise in advance for any omissions. We would be pleased
to insert the appropriate acknowledgments in any subsequent edition of this publication.

CONTENTS

HORSES

Horses are fast, strong and beautiful. A horse galloping across a field will make people stop and watch until the show is over!

Horses are very powerful. We use the word "horsepower" to measure the power of our cars.

We compare a car's power against the natural power of a horse.

HORSES AND HUMANS

Artwork shows that humans have loved horses for thousands of years.

Eventually, humans began taming horses. Groups of people that had horses were faster and stronger than groups that didn't.

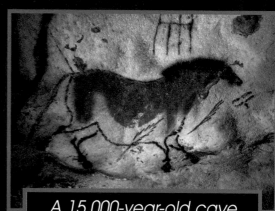

A 15,000-year-old cave painting from France

A piece of ancient Egyptian art showing a horse pulling a chariot. It is over 3,000 years old.

Horses helped people travel farther and for longer periods of time. Once the wheel was invented, horses could pull big loads.

In the Middle Ages, knights rode war horses into battle. A war horse was very expensive. It cost as much as a new car does today!

War horses were trained to kick and bite their knight's enemies.

Knights competed in jousting competitions. They tried to knock each other from their horses using long lances.

A modern-day display of jousting

HORSE BREEDS

People began breeding horses for special uses. Today, there are over 500 different breeds of horses.

The Thoroughbred breed started in England.

A Thoroughbred racehorse

Thoroughbreds were bred to be racehorses. Horses that won races were bred with other winners so that each generation became faster.

Quarter horses were bred in America. They were bred to race and work with cattle.

If running over a quarter of a mile or less, Quarter horses are faster than any other horses in the world.

Quarter horse mare and foal

Arabian horses were bred in Arabia. They were bred to live in the hot, dry desert.

Their coats are fine and silky to help them get rid of heat more easily.

Arabian stallion

LITTLE AND LARGE

Horses come in all sizes, from tiny to gigantic.

Measuring horses

- Horses and ponies are measured in "hands". A hand is 4 inches (10.16 centimetres).

- Horses are measured from the ground to the top of their withers.

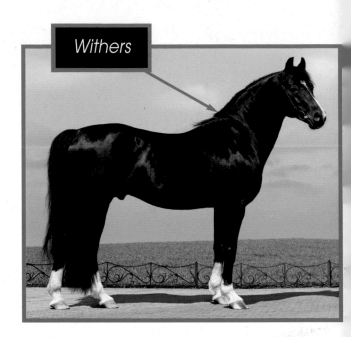

Withers

- A horse is 14 hands 2 inches tall, or taller.

- Ponies are shorter than 14.2 hands.

Thumbelina

Thumbelina is the smallest horse in the world. She is 44.5 centimetres tall – that's just over four hands high!

The largest horse in the world is a Belgium draft horse named Radar.

He is 19 hands 3.5 inches, or 2 metres, tall!

Belgium draft horses are a breed that started in Belgium. They are big, very gentle horses.

This breed was used by knights in the Middle Ages. Today's large, working farm horses were bred from Belgium draft horses.

Radar

HORSE POWER

In the past, horses were power for our heavy machines. They pulled farm machines and fire trucks.

Fire horses gallop to a fire in London in 1910

Harness

When the fire bells rang, experienced fire horses would leave their stalls and stand ready under their harnesses.

The cavalry were army units that used horse power.

Horses carried riders into battle. These horses were called the "light cavalry".

Horse-drawn cannon

Light cavalry horse

The heavy cavalry were the horses that pulled cannons. They also carried soldiers in wagons to the battlefields.

Today, we use jeeps, trucks and tanks to do these jobs.

FARM HORSES

Many small farms still use horse power today.

Horses are more "green" than tractors and oil-powered machines.

Horses can refuel off the land by eating grass and hay.

Their manure is a good fertiliser that helps more crops to grow!

When cutting wood in old forests, some loggers still use horses to remove logs.

Horses are low impact compared to machines. This means they don't hurt the trees that are still growing in the forest. They don't damage the ground or hurt plants and wildlife.

Logger

Horses pulling a plough

POLICE HORSES

Horses are used for police work. Big cities have police officers mounted on horses.

Officers on horseback can see out over crowds. The horses are trained to use their bodies to move crowds of people back.

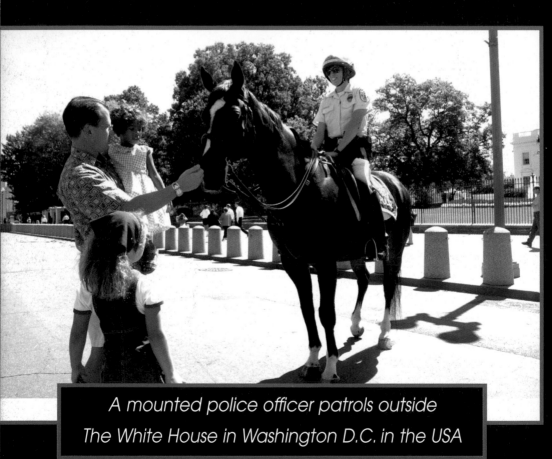

A mounted police officer patrols outside The White House in Washington D.C. in the USA

Police horses can go places cars can't go, such as alleyways and through traffic jams.

The police select horses who are calm and steady.
They are trained for six to 18 months.

A mounted police officer shows that his horse is not afraid of fire during a special display

Police horses are trained to be brave when guns are fired.

They also have to be calm when there is smoke and fire.

MOUNTED POLICE

The Texas Rangers are a law enforcement group in Texas, USA. They use horses in rough country. So do the Royal Canadian Mounted Police, or "Mounties".

If the Texas Rangers or Mounties are looking for a criminal, their horses can go anywhere the criminal goes – and faster!

The Royal Canadian Mounted Police take part in a parade

The horses can also help find a criminal who is hiding.

Horses have a very good sense of smell. A trained horse will point its ears and focus on the place where a person is hiding.

Texas Rangers on patrol in 1915

RACEHORSES

Today, most horses are used for pleasure. Horses are used in many sports, such as racing.

A racehorse can run at over 80 km/h.

From a standing start, a racehorse can outrun a racing car for up to 100 metres.

EVENTING

Eventing is a sport that includes three different tests for a horse and rider.

The sport grew out of the tests that were used to train cavalry riders and their horses.

Test 1

The first test is called a dressage test. The horse must move in straight lines and perfect circles. It must stop exactly on spots marked by big letters.

British rider Zara Phillips with her horse, Toytown

Test 2

The second test is cross-country. The horse and rider gallop across the countryside taking jumps.

They must do this in a set time. Each minute of overtime loses the rider points.

Timber jump

Test 3

The third test is stadium jumping. The horse can touch a jump, but the jump must not fall down.

Post and rail jump

DRIVING HORSES

In carriage driving trials a team of horses pulls a carriage.

The first part of the event is a dressage test. The driver shows how well the horses behave.

Next, is a cross-country drive called the "marathon".

The driver gallops the horses and carriage through gates called "hazards".

Hazard

he hazards are just a little wider than the carriage's wheels. If the driver hits the gates, the carriage might crash or turn over.

The final test is driving through a series of cones with balls balanced on top.

If the horse or the carriage touches a cone, the ball falls off and the team loses points.

RODEO

Rodeo is a popular sport that grew out of ranch work. Cowboys and their horses would compete to show off their skills, such as cutting and roping.

Cutting is how a cowboy gets a cow away from the herd.

A cowboy and cowhorse cutting

Cowhorses are highly trained. They are bred to have "cow sense". This means that they can tell in advance how the cows will move.

When a cow is away from the herd, it can be roped for branding or vaccinations.

Cowboys take part in roping competitions at rodeos.

Roping

Barrel

Barrel racing shows both speed and agility, something cowhorses need.

The horses must gallop around the barrels without knocking them over.

HORSE FOOTBALL

**Football is not just for humans –
horses love it, too!**

Only the horses are allowed to push or kick the ball!

Teams try to push the ball past the other team's goal.

Horses enjoy playing with the ball on their own, too!

NEED TO KNOW WORDS

agility Being able to move, and change position, easily and with speed.

Arabia The area that today is known as the Middle East.

branding Putting a mark on an animal to show who owns it.

bred (to breed) When a male and female animal are put together by humans so that they mate and have young.

breed A type of horse, such as a Thoroughbred or an Arabian.

cavalry An army unit that used soldiers on horseback, or vehicles pulled by horses. Today, cavalry units use machines, such as tanks and helicopters.

fertiliser A substance, such as animal manure, that feeds the soil and makes it better for growing crops.

generation A group of people or animals who are born and live at the same time.

knight A fighting man from the Middle Ages.

Middle Ages The years from around AD 500 to 1500.

ranch A large farm where animals such as cattle and sheep are bred and raised.

taming Making a wild animal friendly and not afraid of humans. A tame animal can be trained.

vaccination An injection that contains a substance which will stop a person or animal catching an illness.

LEARNING TO RIDE

Do you want to learn to ride or drive horses? Search online or look in your local phone book to find riding schools.

Visit several places before you make up your mind. Watch some lessons and ask yourself these questions:

Is everyone wearing helmets?

Is the teacher nice to the students?

Do the horses look well taken care of?

Is the place tidy?

All these things are important if you want to be safe and have fun learning about horses.

HORSES ONLINE

Websites

http://horses4kids.com

http://ultimatehorsefun.com

http://www.youtube.com/watch?v=J5pjxQzb5cE&NR=1

http://www.youtube.com/watch?v=15G2iCYSWP8&

feature=related

INDEX